THE TOM WOLFE TR
75 SANTA PATTERNS

Schiffer Publishing Ltd

Tom Wolfe

4880 Lower Valley Road, Atglen, PA 19310 USA

Book Designed by Bonnie M. Hensley
Typeset in Davida Bd BT/Times New Roman

ISBN: 0-7643-0627-8
Printed in China

Published by Schiffer Publishing Ltd.
4880 Lower Valley Road
Atglen, PA 19310
Phone: (610) 593-1777; Fax: (610) 593-2002
Please write for a free catalog.
This book may be purchased from the publisher.
Please include $3.95 for shipping.

In Europe, Schiffer books are distributed by
Bushwood Books
6 Marksbury Avenue
Kew Gardens
Surrey TW9 4JF England
Phone: 44 (0) 181 392-8585; Fax: 44 (0) 181 392-9876
E-mail: Bushwd@aol.com

Try your bookstore first.

We are interested in hearing from authors
with book ideas on related subjects.

INTRODUCTION

There is always one of three things in my hand: a carving knife, a pencil, or a good cigar. When it's the pencil, I find myself doodling all kinds of characters, many of which find their way into (or out of) the wood.

Some of the favorite characters I draw and carve is Santa Clauses. There is just so much life in them, and they seem to make almost everyone smile. Many of the seventy-five patterns in this book started out as a doodle and have made their way into a carving. They have all kinds of attitudes and positions, and are a great pleasure to carve.

If you are familiar with my work you know that I always give only the side view pattern. Some people figure I'm trying to keep secrets from them, but the truth is that is all I use. The reason is simple. When you try to follow a front pattern and a side pattern the carving almost always gets to looking out of proportion. The life goes out of it!

In my carving books I try to lead the carver step-by-step through the process of taking the figure from a two dimensional pattern to a three dimensional being. I invite you to take a look at those books. You might be especially interested in the companion book to this one *More Santa Carving with Tom Wolfe*, also available from Schiffer Publishing. In the meantime, complete views of finished carvings are given in the back of this book.

I hope you find these patterns fun and useful. As always I welcome your comments.

AMERICAN SANTAS AND ELVES.

I like to do little actions scenes, like this little elf doing a
snowman version of the Boss.

Santa-elves.

Santas at play.

Sometimes I like to do overweight Santas.

Sliding down the hill.

Pickin' up the goodies.

Santa on a stool. This plump Santa on a stool has the seat
carved with the figure and the legs added later.

A leisurely walk in the snow.

The hole seems smaller this year.

A gift to suit a king.

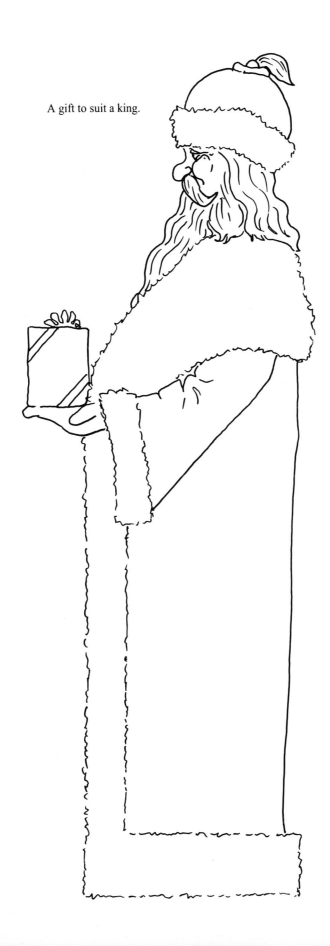

Looks like snow.

Out…

and almost in.

For all the good little pigs in the world.

Reindeer on strike.

Almost done.

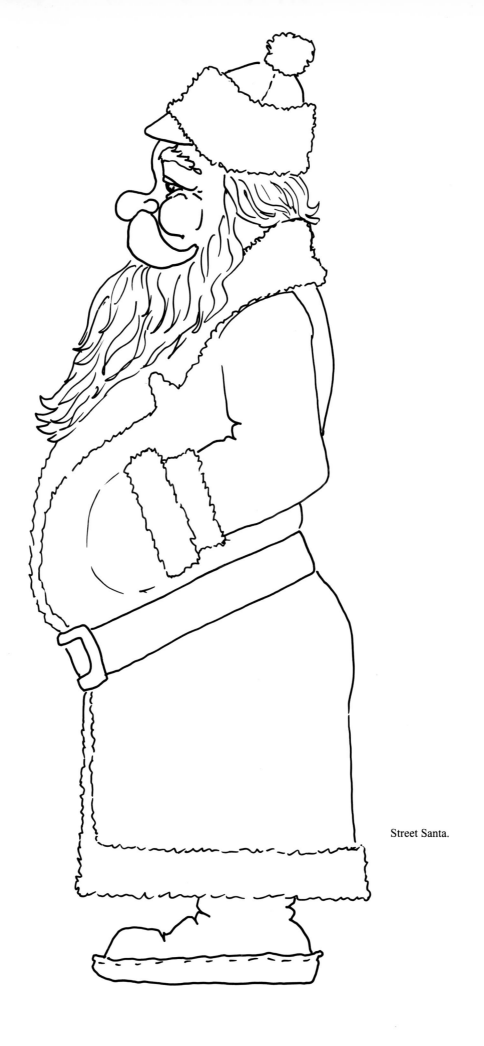

Street Santa.

Mrs. Santa with tea. Any resemblance to a barmaid is unintended!

It's been a long day.

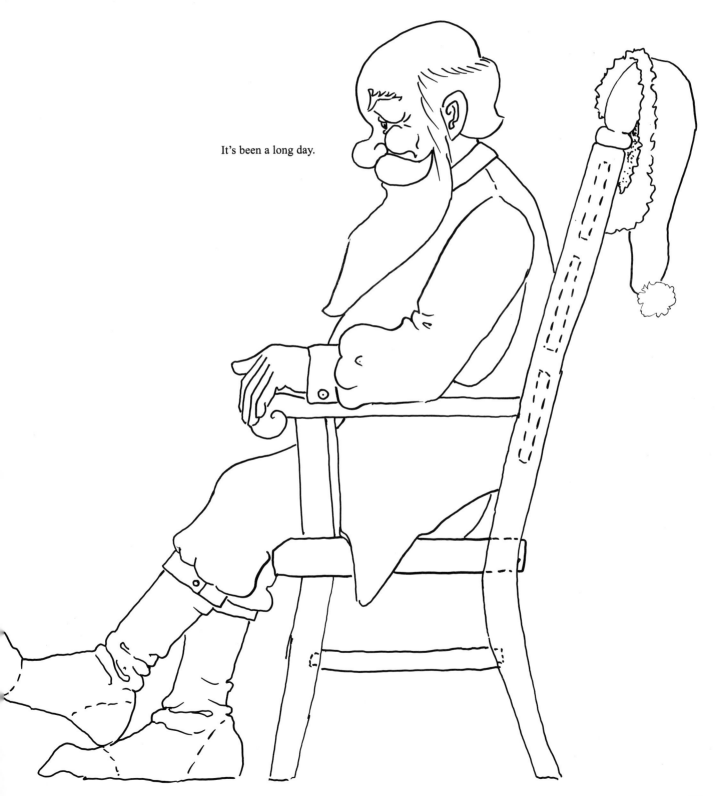

A scooter-puttin' Santa.

A back packing Santa.

A helping hand.

Good cheers and a merry Christmas.

Surfing Santa on a summer sea.

Skating Santa.

Jolly Ol' Santa not so jolly. A pain in the lower lumbar.

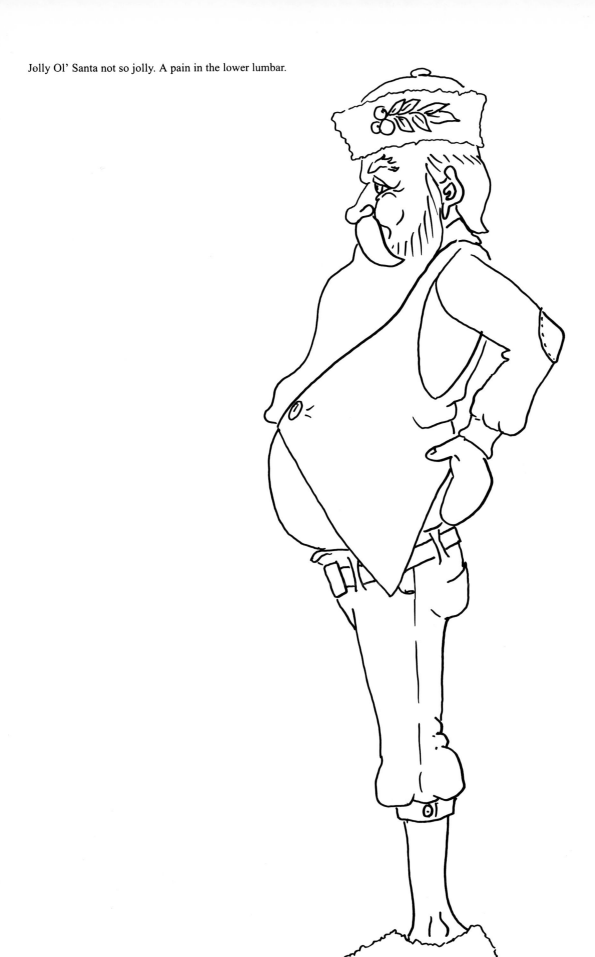

Every toy starts with a design.

Elves just standing around.

This kid's been a pain in the...

The need for speed.

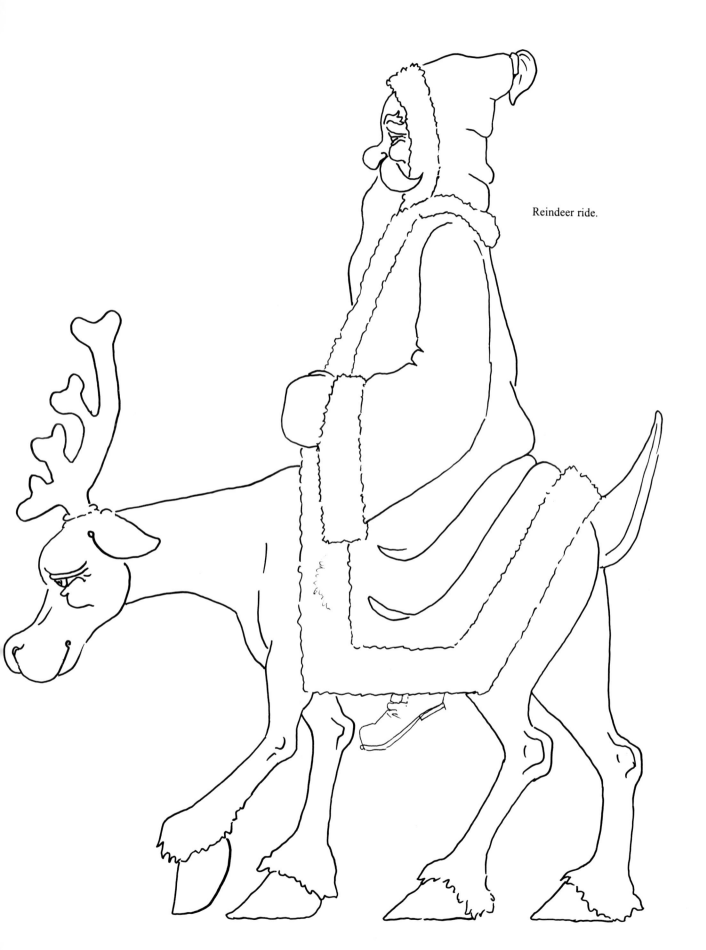

Reindeer ride.

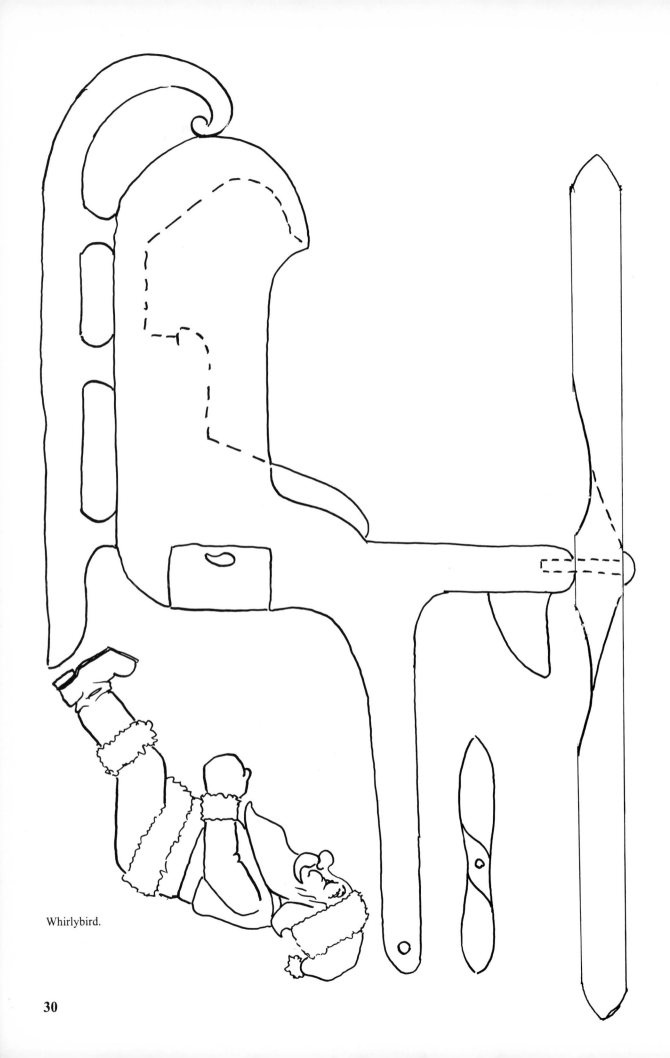

Whirlybird.

Riding the snow goose.

Something for everyone.

Trying out a new model and she's good too!

The three kings.

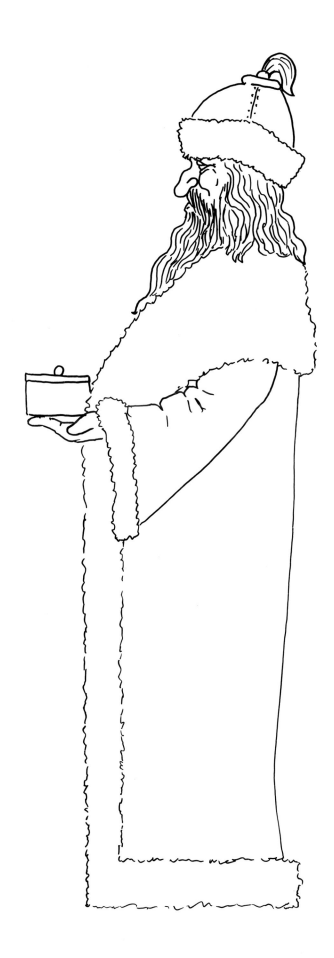

Shepherd looking from afar.

I think a sweet little cherub would look out of place in my book, so
here are some crusty ones.

Garbel and Gabriell.

Gabriell before he grew a beard.

The beginning of a power dive.

I think pigs fly when they die.

Pig angels.

Shelf-sitting Santa

Santa elf.

Kneeling Santa with teddy bear.

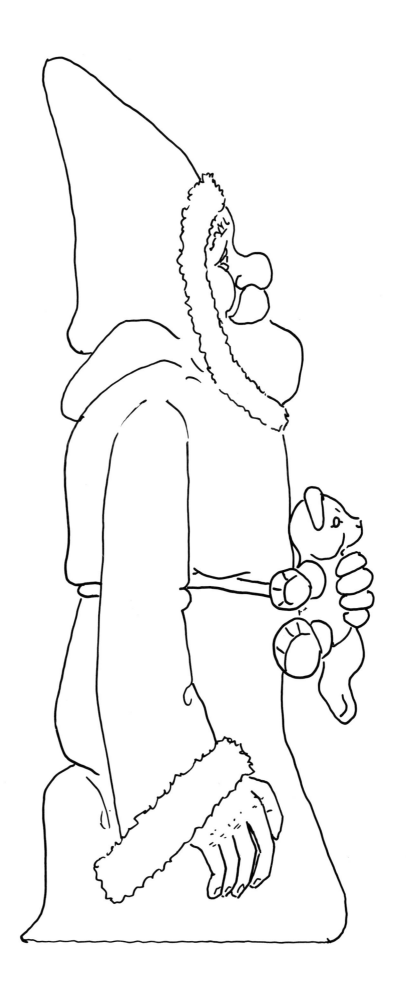

Walking Santa...

Teddy Bear

Inside Santa looking at a bear.

with his dog.

Christmas tree & ornament.

Santa putting the ornament on the tree.

Smokin' Santa.

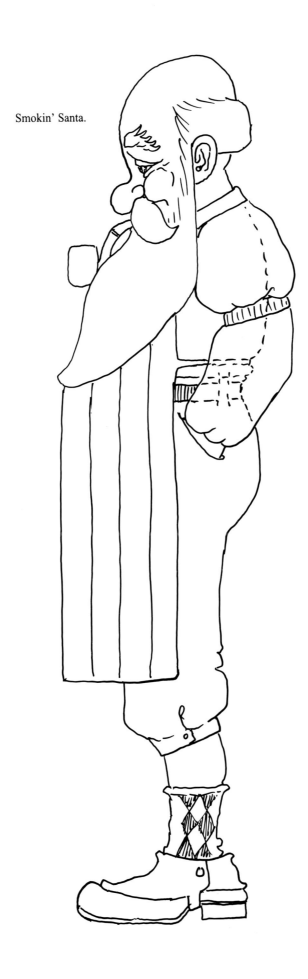

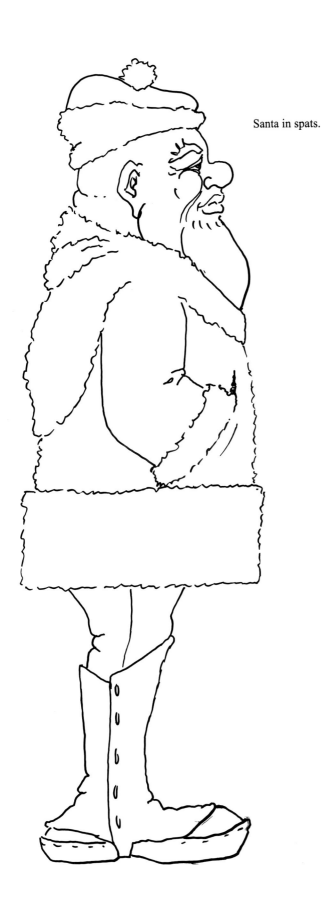

Santa in spats.

Santa looking up, checking the sky.

BUST SECTION

I like to do busts as work studies for pieces.

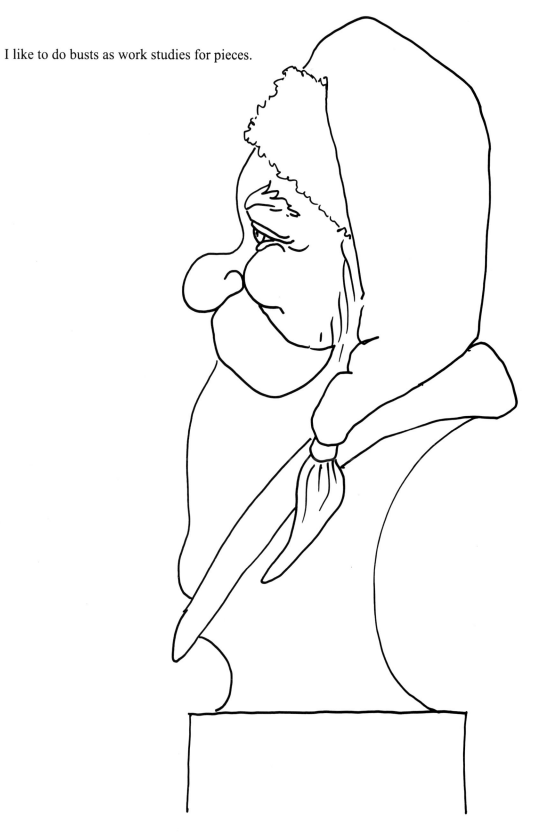

With the tassel over the shoulder it gives this Nick a combination old world-new world look.

Saint Nicholas looking up has a nice spiritual appearance.

Very simple, very loving.

This is an old world Saint Nicholas type. He should look stern, but loveable.

The pattern for this I drew on the computer. It was a lot of fun!

A self portrait. I love kids and never turn down an opportunity to play Santa.

GALLERY

Pattern shown on page 26.

Patterns shown on pages 46 and 47.

Patterns shown on pages 48 and 49.

Patterns shown on pages 48 and 49.

Patterns shown on pages 50 and 51.